the quiet legend:
HENRY AARON

Author

F. M. Milverstedt

Photography

Heinz Kluetmeier

 RAINTREE EDITIONS

Published by   **Raintree Editions**
A Division of Raintree Publishers Ltd.
Milwaukee, Wisconsin 53203

Distributed by   Childrens Press
1224 West Van Buren Street
Chicago, Illinois 60607 ·

Library of Congress Cataloging in Publication Data

Milverstedt, F. M.
    The quiet legend: Henry Aaron

    SUMMARY: A biography of the baseball player who
displaced Babe Ruth as the hitter with the greatest
number of career home runs.
    1. Aaron, Henry, 1934-   —Juvenile literature.
2. Baseball—Juvenile literature. [1. Aaron,
Henry, 1934-   2. Baseball—Biography] I. Kluetmeier, Heinz. II. Title.
GV865.A25M54 1975   796.357'092'4 [B] [92]
ISBN 0-8172-0103-3   75-19277
ISBN 0-8172-0102-5 lib. bdg.

"But prove it, Henry, and thou shalt be king."

— *William Shakespeare*

In the summer of 1975, on a warm and sunny afternoon in Milwaukee, he kneels in the on-deck circle at County Stadium, waiting for his turn at bat.

His surroundings are familiar. He has been here before, gone away and returned. In a sense, he has come back home.

The team and the uniforms are new, the league is different. But the feel of the stadium has not changed.

It is more than just the sights and sounds and smells. It is more than the spike-scarred dugouts, the red and green wooden seats, and the gray steel beams of the grandstands. It is more than the press box, the flashing scoreboard in center field, the signs and pennants in the bleachers, or the vendors hawking their bratwursts and beer.

It is the feeling of this city, the feeling of these fans. It is a feeling that has not changed with the passing of a decade.

He played in this city for 12 seasons. He arrived here as a rookie in 1954. He remained until 1965, the year the owners of the Milwaukee Braves moved the team to Atlanta.

The years here were good. He remembers them fondly.

In 1954, Milwaukee was a ballplayer's dream, a rookie's paradise. The Braves had been here for only one year. They had moved west from Boston in the first of several major

league franchise shifts. The city was overjoyed. The Braves would put Milwaukee on the map, bring it the trappings of big league status. The entire State of Wisconsin was in love with baseball.

The players were welcomed with open arms, cheered mightily, taken to the hearts of their fans like adopted children. Win or lose, they were the favored sons.

It was the perfect setting for an inexperienced youngster, an unpolished rookie in his third season of professional ball. It was a place to gain confidence, develop skills, and move toward maturity.

He moved at his own pace, quickly picking up speed, and the fans cheered him on.

In his first year as a Brave, he started in the outfield and hit .280.

By 1956, he was the National League batting champion,

hitting .328. He led the league in hits, total bases, and doubles. He hit 26 home runs.

The following season, he led the Braves to the pennant and a World Series victory. He was the National League's Most Valuable Player. He was the league leader in home runs, hits, total bases, and runs batted in.

The championship was greeted by the wildest celebration in the history of Milwaukee. The Braves were honored as never before, and the young man with the perfect swing stood first among them.

In 1958, he helped the team to a second straight pennant. Although a bit of the glitter was dulled by a World Series defeat, he had another bright season. He batted .326, with 30 home runs.

Another batting title followed in 1959. He hit .355 and brought the Braves to within one game of a third straight pennant. They lost it in a playoff with the Los Angeles Dodgers in the 12th inning.

Over the course of the next six seasons, he averaged .317 and knocked in 715 runs. He hit 219 homers.

Milwaukee marveled at his talent. He was the backbone of the Braves, a local idol, and the pride of the community.

But slowly the love affair began to fade. The club was taken over by new men, people who had not been present in the idyllic beginning. They made changes in the team that were unpopular with the fans. The Braves' playing fell off, and so did attendance at their games. The club started losing money.

The new owners began to look elsewhere for profit. They looked to the untapped market of the deep South, and they settled on Atlanta, virgin land to big league baseball.

By the close of the 1965 season, the Braves had moved once more. Milwaukee was abandoned.

But for the all-star outfielder, there was little outward change.

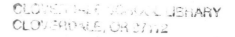

In Atlanta, closer to his roots and birthplace in Mobile, his play remained outstanding. His skills increased, his reputation grew. Over the next nine years, he rewrote the record books.

In 21 total seasons in the major leagues, he accumulated over 3,000 hits, one of only 10 players in the history of the game to do so. In 14 of those seasons, he batted over .300. In eight, he hit 40 or more home runs. '

He collected the most total bases, most extra base hits, most sacrifice flies, most bases on balls, most runs batted in. And . . . the record they will always remember . . . most home runs.

He became the greatest slugger the sport has ever known. His career has no equal.

It reached its peak on the night of April 8, 1974, in the fourth inning of a game with the Los Angeles Dodgers in Atlanta Stadium. On a one-and-oh pitch, he stepped into an Al Downing fast ball, snapped his wrists, and whipped his bat around. He connected solidly, driving the ball hard over the fence in left-center field.

It was his 715th lifetime home run. It was the home run that broke Babe Ruth's record.

He was the man of the hour. He was hailed across the country, toasted and cheered by millions. He was mobbed by interviewers and agents. He signed a million dollar contract to do public relations work for a television manufacturer.

But after the uproar had died down, after the season was over, he shook the baseball world by asking for a trade. He wanted to return to Milwaukee. There was a new team there, the Brewers, and he said he wanted to be part of it.

Over the years, little by little, his relationship with the Braves' management had cooled.

He once had hopes of managing the team when his playing career had ended. The club owners were aware of his desire,

but they had other ideas. They were content to use him as an attendance draw, a player the fans would pay to see. But that was as far as it went.

He stayed with the club out of loyalty, determined to break Ruth's record in the uniform of the team that had given him his start. But once that milestone was achieved, he was prepared to take his leave.

In Atlanta, he saw no future. In Milwaukee, he recognized a place that was secure.

"I was not out for the highest bidder," he said later. "I wanted the Brewers. I told my attorney that the only club I wanted to be with was the Milwaukee Brewers.

"I dreamed someday that I'd come back to Milwaukee and finish my career there. I'm happy my dream came true."

His return to Milwaukee was celebrated in a splash of pomp and public attention. He had come home, and the city and the state welcomed him warmly.

For the Brewers, a young club struggling for respectability, he was a godsend.

Together with his manager, Del Crandall, his teammate on the Braves during the glory years, he would bring to the Brewers a spirit of the old Milwaukee.

He would fuse relations between the club and the city. He would be the biggest gate attraction in the game. His booming bat would increase the Brewers' run production. He would lend a calm leadership to the younger players around him.

He was wiser now. He had matured. He could look back on his life and reflect, lending his experience.

He had been modest and shy for all of his life. But the flood of attention he attracted during his run for Ruth's record had made him more at ease, more willing to talk out about his thoughts and habits, his opinions and ideals.

In the spring, at the Brewer training camp in Sun City, Arizona, he met with the team at Crandall's request and spoke of his ideas. Later, he talked with reporters.

"I imagine a lot of them think that it was easy for me because I've been blessed with talent," he said. "But it wasn't easy, and I told them.

"I spoke of the adjustments I had to make in my career— of the dedication and discipline I developed through the years. If I hadn't done all those things and made adjustments, I would have been out of baseball eight years ago.

"I talked to them about concentration and discipline, how to make adjustments and not waste all of those years without doing it.

"I told them to keep their composure in situations where they'll look bad, and not throw a helmet to the ground or break a bat. There were many times when I'd get mad, but I'd get back to the dugout and rationalize and get my composure back.

"I know how frustrating it can be for a young kid. He loses his composure. You have to drill it in their minds that they're young and they can learn from their mistakes.

"Progress," he said, "comes from the ability to learn."

In the on-deck circle, his pose is relaxed. He leans on his bat, his chin resting on his hands.

He is poised, in tune with the game. Beneath the blue visor of his batting helmet, his clear brown eyes are attentive, his mind alert. He is watching the pitcher, studying each motion, recording each pitch.

The American League is unfamiliar. He has played in it for only part of a season. He is still learning the styles of different pitchers, observing their strengths, discovering their weaknesses.

This one is a tall right-hander, hard-throwing and a little wild, a youngster with a strong arm and a problem with control. On a one-and-one count, he comes in quick with a fast ball. It tails away, just missing the outside corner.

A fast ball.

It is unlikely that he will see one himself when he steps to the plate. They don't often throw that kind of pitch to the most respected fast ball hitter in the game. Mostly, they just throw him junk.

He has not hit it well. The season has been disappointing. Beneath the quiet exterior, he is impatient. He is going through a time of adjustment.

As the Brewers' designated hitter, he no longer takes his turn in the field. At the age of 41, his arm no longer has the snap for hard, quick throws from the outfield. The years of wear on his legs have slowed his speed. His job now is only to hit.

But he is not yet familiar with the American League umpires or the strike zones they prefer. He has not yet learned the habits of the pitchers he must face.

He has been handicapped by the weaker Brewer hitters in the lineup. He has had to face men on the mound who are very willing to take the time to pitch around him. They offer little in the way of meaty pitches, trying instead to retire him with off-speed curves and changes, pitching the spots.

His batting average has hovered near .230. The home runs have been few. With runners on base, he has not hit with the consistency that once was his trademark.

He bears these problems quietly. He knew that these things could happen when he made his decision to shift to the American League. He knows they must happen with each aging year.

He can only bide his time and try his best, hoping for the hits to fall. He can only wait it out, letting nature and his talent take their course.

To the public and the other players, he has nothing left to

prove. He has reached a level of achievement that others only dream of.

He is a wealthy man. He is famous. He has pursued his playing career to its highest. But still he seeks to excel.

It is chiefly a matter of pride.

He has pride in himself, a quality that has always driven him to greater heights. He has pride in these fans, pride in this city, pride in this state. He holds them each in honor. He has chosen to be one of them.

In the days when he was young and unsure of himself, a poor boy from Alabama, alone and far from his home, they accepted him, watched him with admiration as he grew to be a man. They respected him, and they treated him fairly.

In these, the final years of his playing career, he will share with them his glory.

He will do what he can, as well as he can, for as long as he can, for he knows no other way.

The hitter walks. The crowd stirs, cheering, even before his name is announced. He rises from the on-deck circle and moves slowly toward the plate, ambling, his bat held lightly in his hand.

"Now batting, for Milwaukee, Number 44 . . . Henry Aaron!"

The stadium erupts. Ushers, vendors, and police, everyone joins in the applause. It is this way every time he comes to bat. Thousands of people are clapping, shouting, clambering to their feet in tribute.

He moves into the batter's box, hands raised to his helmet, fitting it secure. He positions his feet and taps his bat once upon the plate. He raises the bat to his shoulders, coiling it behind his right ear, hands held in close. He turns to face the pitcher.

The cheering continues, swelling, rippling through the stands, echoing in every corner of the stadium.

It is the praise reserved for only a few. It is the praise accorded to heroes.

In the eyes of most Americans, Henry Aaron was not a likely hero.

He did not reflect the proper image. He was not in line with a tradition. He was, in fact, at odds with history.

Henry Aaron had talent. He won countless games with his bat and glove. He set records. But in spite of these achievements, he never received much attention. For most of his career, in the eyes of most Americans, he was all but ignored.

In a way, it all began with Babe Ruth.

It began in 1920, the year the New York Yankees bought Ruth from the Boston Red Sox. Ruth was a pitcher then, a left-hander and a good one, but it was his bat the Yankees wanted.

In 1919, playing field and pitching for the Red Sox, he had hit 29 home runs, an astonishing figure for the time.

It was only a hint of what was to come.

In his first season with the Yankees, Ruth hit 54 home runs. In the next 15 years, he was the most powerful hitter in baseball. His yearly home run totals sometimes exceeded the totals of whole teams.

Ruth revolutionized baseball. He changed the strategy from

defense to offense, resolving the outcome of a game with a single swing of his bat. Huge crowds turned out to watch him, and with the crowds came a new popularity for baseball and a new prosperity for the players and owners.

Ruth turned the game into an American institution, the showcase of a nation.

In 1919, the country had been shocked to find out that members of the Chicago White Sox had tried to "throw" the World Series to gamblers. In the wake of this "Black Sox Scandal," Ruth was hailed as a savior.

He took to his role with gusto. He played it to the hilt. There had never been anyone like him in baseball before.

His batting record was monumental: a .342 lifetime average, 2,209 runs batted in, and the incredible total of 714 home runs.

714 home runs.

It was a record, they said, that would never be broken.

But it was not only what Ruth did that made him memorable. It also was the time in which he did it, and the way in which he went about it.

He responded to the needs of a nation, and he did it with a flair.

In the 1920s, America was in search of a direction, in search of a clear self-image, in search of a hero. The frontiers had been conquered and closed. World War I had been won. For the first time in their short history, Americans had time on their hands and the desire to put it to use.

They began to take a closer look at who they were and what they were made of. In their examination, they found limitless energy and an urge to let off steam.

And in Babe Ruth, they found much to be said of themselves.

He was a simple man, blessed with good humor, a huge appetite, and a love for children. Strong and powerfully built, he had the soul of an overgrown boy.

He had an eye for the dramatic, sometimes in laughter, sometimes in tears. He was loud and boisterous, quick with his money, slow to leave a bar or the side of a fun-loving friend. He was a lover of the good life.

The unwanted son of a poor man, he had been raised in a Baltimore orphanage and he had made it to the top on his own. He was earning $80,000 a year and dining with princes, all for the sake of hitting a small ball great distances with a powerful swing of a large wooden stick.

Babe Ruth was proof that the system worked. He was proof that in America, if nowhere else on earth, a poor boy, homeless and uneducated, could put his special talent to work and rise up to touch at the stars.

In the eyes of his public, he was a god who walked among men. But beneath it all, he also was a human being with whom they could identify.

He was the spirit of the Roaring Twenties. He was the symbol of a culture. He was the American Dream come true.

The dream ended in 1935, the year that Ruth retired. The high life of the Roaring Twenties had vanished. In its place was the Great Depression.

It was a time of fear. Jobs were scarce, and money was tight. There was little to depend on, little that had not changed for the worse.

Baseball was one of the few remnants of better days. It was something to be counted on. It was the Great American Game, complete with Great American Idols.

Ruth was gone, and there would never be another like him. But there would be those who followed. Like Ruth, they would be symbols of their place and time.

The first would be Joe DiMaggio.

In 1936, when DiMaggio joined the Yankees as their rookie

center fielder, the mood of the nation was sober and serious, sensible and hard-working.

DiMaggio shared these values. In his quiet and determined way, he gained the admiration and respect of his fellow Americans. He was someone they could count on.

While America was staggering through the Depression, the New York Yankees kept right on winning, just as they had under Ruth. In a time of uncertainty, the Yankees were a constant. And it was DiMaggio who led the way.

They called him, "the Yankee Clipper."

He moved with the grace of a sailing ship and he made impossible plays look easy. In the field, he always made the catch, no matter how hard. At bat, he was the steadiest hitter in the game.

In perhaps his greatest feat, in 1941, he hit safely in 56 consecutive games.

Through the years of World War II, and through the early years of peace, it was DiMaggio who caught the imagination of a nation. It was DiMaggio who stood as the symbol of a decade.

His fame would never equal Ruth's, but like Ruth, he would leave a permanent mark. He would never be surpassed, he could only be replaced.

And in 1951, the year that he retired, there was a chosen successor in the dugout. His name was Mickey Mantle. The dugout was in Kansas City, the Triple-A Yankee farm club in the American Association.

He was 20 years old, three years out of high school, and he was hitting .361.

They said he was another DiMaggio. They said he had the power to beat Ruth, that he hit the ball a mile. They said he was the fastest man in baseball, and they said he was the strongest.

They made him the heir to the legend. Suddenly, almost overnight, America had another baseball idol.

In the eyes of most Americans, he was the perfect model for the time. He was the all-American boy.

He came out of the country's heartland, a little Oklahoma town called Commerce. In the rush and bustle of a place like New York City, he was like a babe in the woods.

He was a bit of a yokel, humble and very shy, and he seldom spoke. When he did, it was usually something like, "Aw, shucks."

If he smoked or drank, no one ever knew. Instead, he chewed gum, blowing big pink bubbles in the outfield.

He was clean-shaven. He wore his blond hair in a crewcut.

He was young, well-built, and, in a boyish sort of way, he was handsome. He looked exactly like everyone's idea of a high school football star. Which, in fact, he was.

He was the face of a nation.

And there was one more thing, a very important thing that cannot be overlooked: Like Ruth, like DiMaggio, like all the other American heroes who had come before, he was the son of a white man.

America was a white man's country. White men founded it, and white men made the rules. White men were its only heroes.

In 180 years of American history, there was no other way, there were no other models.

For one like Henry Aaron, a black man in a white man's game, the praise accorded to heroes would be a long time in coming.

In 1934, the year that Henry Aaron was born, blacks in America were only 71 years removed from slavery.

The Emancipation Proclamation had broken their bonds, but they still were not free. They still were not equal.

At the very best, they were second-class citizens.

Blacks hardly ever owned land. They often were not allowed to vote. Their chances for a good education were small.

Black people could be servants, tenant farmers, porters or domestics, hired hands, or laborers. Perhaps, if they were quick of wit, if they could dance or sing, they could be entertainers. If they tried to be more, they could get in trouble.

The discrimination could be both subtle and violent. It might be a door slammed in a black person's face or a curse shouted his way. Or it might be a pounding on the door in the dead of night, the terror of a lynch mob.

Sports offered little, almost nothing.

Before the turn of the century, jockeys in horse racing often were black. But as the sport became more popular, they were replaced by whites. Boxing held some small promise, but only two people really made it to the top — Jack

Johnson and Joe Louis. In track and field, there was only Jesse Owens.

Professional football and basketball were not very popular. Tennis and golf and swimming were the sports of the rich.

Blacks were barred from baseball.

It was nothing official, they simply weren't hired by major league teams. It wasn't heard of, it wasn't even thought of. If blacks wanted to play baseball, it was understood, they had their own leagues to play in.

All of that changed in 1947, when Branch Rickey, general manager of the Brooklyn Dodgers, signed a young black second baseman by the name of Jackie Robinson. Rickey knew that it took talent to win championships. For the talent he saw in Jackie Robinson, he was willing to break the color barrier.

Robinson never had it easy. He was a marked man. He was

the target of insults and taunts from fans and rival players. He bore the weight of a country's eyes upon him. He was the representative of an entire race.

He took the role as a challenge. He hit the major leagues in a cloud of dust and a flash of spikes, and he played as hard as he could. He was the most competitive man in the game. He fought every inch of the way, stealing a base, bouncing back from a knock-down pitch, breaking up the double-play.

In time, he became the pride of the Dodgers. Because of his example, other blacks were soon to follow.

By the early 1950s, black men were slowly breaking into the lineups of most major league teams. There was Satchel Paige, Luke Easter, and Larry Doby in Cleveland; Joe Black and Don Newcombe in Brooklyn; Minnie Minoso and Ernie Banks in Chicago; Sam Jethroe and Jim Pendleton in Boston; Monte Irvin and Hank Thompson in New York.

And in Milwaukee, there was Henry Aaron.

No one paid too much attention to him when he first reported to the Milwaukee training camp at Bradenton, Florida, in the spring of 1954, but he was used to being ignored. A lean and wide-eyed rookie, he stayed to himself, kept his mouth closed. He let his skill speak for him.

As a boy, growing up in Mobile, playing ball was about the only thing that ever really interested him. He loved to play and he was good at it, even though he had the peculiar habit of batting with a cross-handed grip.

He was 13 years old when Jackie Robinson first hit the big leagues, and from that time on, he knew what he wanted from life.

He wanted to be a major league ballplayer. He knew he had the talent, he knew that he could do it. He made up his mind that he would.

Since his high school had no baseball team, he started

playing softball. He played it on the playgrounds and the sandlots, and he played it pretty well.

He caught the attention of a local scout by the name of Ed Scott, who offered him $10 to play on weekends for the Black Bears, a Mobile semi-pro team. His mother said no, because he'd be playing on Sunday, but the young man wouldn't give up. He said it was important, and finally his mother gave in. He was 17 years old.

He was playing infield then, mostly third base and shortstop. He had a lot to learn about how to play the field. He was crude, and he threw with a funny kind of underhand motion. But even with that awkward cross-handed grip, at the plate he was a hitter.

He was a natural.

In later years, he would work to improve his talent. He would develop his wrists, and practice his timing, and keep his body fit and in good health. But always, he would follow his natural rhythms, waiting for his pitch, swinging freely when it came.

His hitting soon caught the attention of the Indianapolis Clowns, a barnstorming black club that never got much closer to Indianapolis than a cheap hotel on the south side of Chicago. They lived out of suitcases, traveled and slept on rickety old buses, and ate their meals from paper sacks they filled along the way at rundown roadside stops.

They were shabby, but they were a one-way ticket out of Mobile. When the Clowns asked him to sign, Henry was ready to ride.

His stay with the Clowns was short, just about long enough to straighten out the cross-handed grip. It was the only time in his career when anyone would tamper with his style.

A few weeks after he joined the Clowns, Henry was spotted by a Boston Braves scout, a man named Dewey Griggs. On the night in Buffalo, New York, that Griggs watched a

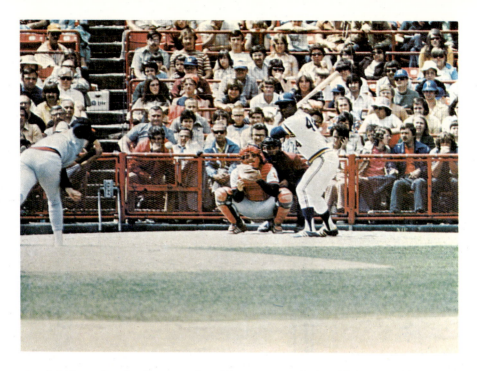

doubleheader between the Clowns and the Kansas City Monarchs, Aaron went seven-for-nine. He hit a home run over the left field fence and another over the right.

The Braves bought him from the Clowns for $2,500 and an option. If they didn't like him, they could send him back. If he made it to the big leagues, Syd Pollock, the Clowns' owner, would receive another $7,500. When Aaron left the club, Pollock gave him a cardboard suitcase.

Aaron spent 1952 in the Northern League, in a town called Eau Claire in central Wisconsin, not too far from the Mississippi River. He had never been north before, he had never lived with whites, and he was lonely.

After just two weeks in town, he was ready to call it quits and go back home. He phoned to tell them he was coming, but his brother, Herbert, talked him into staying.

The summer turned out well. He combed the Class C pitching for an average of .336, second in the league, and he collected 116 hits. He was selected to the All-Star team and was named Rookie of the Year. He was on his way.

But first, there was a stop in Jacksonville.

The Braves had taken a look at him early in the spring of 1953, but they said he wasn't quite ready. They said he couldn't pull the ball. They wanted to give him more seasoning.

In Jacksonville, he got his seasoning.

He had a fantastic year. He was named the Most Valuable Player, batted .362, knocked in 125 runs, hit 22 homers, and led the league in five categories.

But there was something else. He would run into it again, 20 years later, when his quest for Ruth's record had captured the attention of the entire nation. But in 1953, he was seeing it for the first time.

It was racial hatred.

It wasn't something found only in the South. The entire country was painfully slow in adjusting to integration. It remains so to this day. But in the South, where the labor of black slaves was the key to a whole economy and culture, the fires of prejudice were still burning fiercely.

The Sally League, with franchises in Georgia, South Carolina, Alabama, and Florida, was the last league in professional baseball to allow blacks to play.

The first three blacks all played for Jacksonville: Horace Garner, Felix Mantilla, and Henry Aaron.

It was an experience Henry would always remember.

He was no stranger to segregation. He had grown up with it in Mobile, and it followed him through his early springs in the South with the Braves. He knew about discrimination. His father was a boilermaker's helper in a shipyard, thankful for the job.

But he was astounded that people could hate him for no

more than the color of his skin, that he could be booed for no more than playing a game on the same field as white men.

Jacksonville itself was not so bad. The team had a large following of black fans, and there was no tension. It was out on the road, on hot and dusty nights in Georgia and Alabama, where he saw the bitterness.

It came at him in doses large and small.

It was a challenge from the bleachers in Montgomery, a hoarse voice calling, "Nigger!"

It was a brawl on the field in Macon, with fans and police spilling out of the stands.

It was the restaurants where he could not eat, the hotel clerks who would not rent him a room, the separate quarters for black players and white.

It was a fire growing dimmer, but it singed him with its heat. The embers glow today, the flame has left a mark.

In later years, he would look back on that time. He would see it not so much for the unpleasantness, as for the fact that it was a sign of the South opening up, a sign that America itself was slowly giving the black person his due.

He would watch black people's progress, slow but sure, for the rest of his life.

But in 1953, at the age of 19, there was much about life he did not understand.

Even as he wondered, hurt and bewildered, he kept it to himself. He would never be a politician. He would never be a crusader for equal rights or black militancy. He would never point to bigotry as an excuse for his limitations.

He would go about his own quiet way, with pride and dignity, but always with modesty. He would demand nothing for himself but respect as a human being and the right to go about his business. He would seek no more attention than what his bat could command.

He would play baseball.

32

In his first three seasons in the major leagues, Henry Aaron would become one of the most respected hitters in the game.

By 1957, he would be the National League's Most Valuable Player. He would play in one All-Star game after another. Over the next 17 years, he would clinch his place in the Hall of Fame.

But it would take a while for Americans to fully understand how good he was. For many years, he would perform in the shadow of others.

Mickey Mantle would be one, and Willie Mays would be the other.

Willie Mays was baseball's first widely popular black star. When Aaron and the others were breaking in, Mays was already famous.

Like Aaron, he grew up in a poor family. He lived in the North, in New York City. While Aaron was playing softball on the playground, he was playing stick ball in the streets.

He was a colossal hitter, both for power and for average. He was quick, he took chances, he had a rifle arm, and he wove a web of magic with his glove.

He came to the New York Giants after a hot start with Minneapolis in the American Association, batting .477. He

lost a year to the Army, but when he returned, he hit .345 and led the Giants to the championship of baseball.

He did it with a style that was sensational.

There were some who called it showboating, the way he raced all over the field, leaping and tumbling and losing his cap. There were some who waited for the day when he would try his basket catch, his glove held low at his waist, and the ball would hit him on the head.

But it never did. Like DiMaggio, he always made the catch.

He made one at the Polo Grounds in the '54 World Series that will never be forgotten. It capped a fantastic season, and it made him an instant star.

Vic Wertz of Cleveland was batting. He hit one to the deepest part of center field, over 500 feet from home plate. There was a pocket out there, a wide recession in the wall that led to the club house.

Mays started running with the crack of the bat. He turned his back and raced deep into the pocket, legs churning, his cap flying off his head. At the last instant, he threw a quick glance over his shoulder at the ball, reached out in front of him like a football pass receiver, and hauled it in.

It was not long after that they wrote a song about him. They called it, "Say-Hey Willie."

He became the "Say-Hey Kid." The people of New York fell in love with him. He had come from their city, and they were proud to tell the world. His name was known across the nation.

It was much the same for Mantle.

From 1953 to the end of the decade, with Mantle providing the big power on the hardest-hitting team in baseball, the Yankees only lost the pennant twice. They won it five more times between 1960 and 1964.

In the field, he was not as flashy as Mays, but he still was a

great defensive player and often made spectacular catches of his own. As a slugger, he was awesome.

He would not just hit home runs, he would hit towering drives. He would hit them so high that they would drop into the stands like mortar shells.

He once hit a home run in Washington that traveled over 560 feet. He hit another in Yankee Stadium that came within a foot of clearing the grandstand roof, something that no one else, not even Ruth, had ever done before.

In 1956, the year that Aaron won his first batting championship, Mantle won the American League Triple Crown, leading the league in average, runs batted in, and homers. He hit 52 home runs that year. They said if his legs held out, he would someday break Ruth's record.

But his legs would prove his downfall. For all of the strength in his upper body, his legs were very brittle. As a youth, he had a bone disease. Combined with an endless string of pulls

and sprains, breaks and tears, he was often hobbled.

The news out of New York about his legs was almost as common as the news about his home runs.

But in 1956, his legs were fine and the country was his playground. That was the year they wrote a song about him. It was called, "I Love Mickey."

Like Mays, he was an almost instant superstar. When fans talked about the greatest player in baseball, it always came down to Mantle or Mays.

For Henry Aaron, as good as he was, there was only the role of a talented also-ran. He was mentioned by some, but seldom in the same breath as Mantle or Mays. He was never seen as any better than third best.

There were some other good ballplayers as well. Roberto Clemente would sometimes get a mention, or maybe Frank Robinson, or Ernie Banks, or Warren Spahn, or later Sandy

Koufax. Old-timers would say that Ted Williams and Stan Musial in their prime were better than them all. But none of them had the glamor of Mantle or Mays, and none of them played in New York.

New York was the nation's largest city, and the place where stars were born. Anyplace else was out in left field.

While Aaron was playing in Milwaukee, establishing his reputation in the hinterlands of Wisconsin, Mantle and Mays were performing daily for the largest TV and radio audiences in the world.

Milwaukee might as well have been a village on the Rhine for the dent it made in national interest. It was too far removed from the limelight. The Yankees said as much when they arrived there for the 1957 Series and called it, "bush."

But for eight glorious days in October, Aaron and the Braves made them eat their words.

The '57 Braves were a powerful club that had everything. Under the management of Fred Haney, stern but fair, and wise in the ways of baseball, the Braves were the end product of a five-year effort by their owners to rule the game.

Along with Aaron, there were solid hitters like Eddie Mathews, Joe Adcock (before he broke a leg), Frank Torre, Red Schoendienst, and Bob "Hurricane" Hazle, who came on late in the season to wield a hot bat when some of the others were slumping.

The pitching staff was tight, headed by Spahn, Lew Burdette, and Bob Buhl. Defensively, they had great strength up the middle, with Del Crandall catching, Schoendienst and Johnny Logan playing shortstop and second base, and Billy Bruton playing center field.

They had won the pennant late in the season in a hot race with the St. Louis Cardinals. They clinched it against the Cards on the night of Sept. 23, in the 11th inning at

Milwaukee County Stadium, when Aaron homered over the center field fence with a man on base.

The Series was a seesaw battle that went the full seven games. Burdette won three of them, including a 5-0 shutout. And Aaron was nearly perfect.

There had been some talk before the Series about a match-up between Mantle and Aaron. The sportswriters agreed that each was the class of his club, but in a vote to predict who would be the Series hero, Mantle won going away.

It was not to be. Mantle started well, but was injured in the third game and appeared only now and then in the final four. But even if he had been in top form, he probably could not have matched the pace that Aaron set.

In the seven games, Aaron had 11 hits, for an average of .393. He hit three homers, drove in seven runs, and collected 22 total bases.

In 1958, the Braves won another pennant, but lost the Series to the Yankees in six games. In 1959, they tied for the National League championship with the Dodgers, but lost it in a playoff.

Briefly, for those three seasons, the Braves and Henry Aaron were national news. But after the pennants had come and gone, they were quickly forgotten. The team slipped into the second division. Except for two contending years after the move to Atlanta, the Braves never again came close to a championship.

The national spotlight returned to New York, to San Francisco and Los Angeles, to Mantle and Mays, to the Dodgers and later the Mets. Henry Aaron returned to his place in the wings of the stage.

In moving from Milwaukee to Atlanta, Aaron traded a rural outpost in the Midwest for the model city of the New South. Atlanta was a hustling, bustling place where people were just a little too concerned with progress and making money to become too excited about major league baseball. In neither city did he find a national showcase for his skills, not for many seasons, not until it became clear that he was closing in on Babe Ruth's record.

But even if he had played in New York, Aaron might not have attracted the attention of the press and public any sooner than he did in Milwaukee or Atlanta.

They said that he lacked color.

He didn't have the style or personality of Mays. He didn't have the mystique of Mantle.

He didn't hit home runs a mile into the air. He hit them on low line shots, screamers that flew off his bat like hard singles over the infield but just kept ripping until they landed in the seats. He hit so many that way that for years no one really thought he was a home run hitter.

He didn't rush all over the field on defense, falling down or making sliding catches. He did these things once in awhile, but only when he couldn't get to the ball gracefully, at his own normal pace.

He didn't have bad legs. He didn't pal around with the press, cracking jokes or making controversial statements that made good copy. He wasn't glamorous and he was born too soon to join the wave of rebels who began to crowd professional sport in the '60s.

He was so colorless, in fact, that in his early years with Milwaukee, his manager, Charlie Grimm, would make up stories that made him sound like a comedian, just so the newspapers would have something to print.

The Braves' publicity people made up a nickname for him. They called him "Hammerin' Hank," and, in later years, "the Hammer."

But it was the ballplayers themselves who would finally give him a name that had the right ring. They would speak it in dugouts and bullpens throughout baseball. They would speak it with a respectful mixture of awe and wry humor.

They would call him, "Bad Henry."

He would stand in a class of his own.

Mantle would be the first to fall by the wayside. He would never catch Ruth, neither in total home runs nor runs in a single season. He would come close to one mark—he would hit 54 homers in 1961. But in the same year, his teammate, Roger Maris, would break Ruth's single season record with 61.

Mantle's legs would crumble by the mid-1960s. The pain would get worse and he would be injured more often. He would retire with 536 home runs.

Mays would last longer. He would move with the Giants to San Francisco and he would wind down his career in windswept Candlestick Park. He would blast 666 home runs, but his

body would fail him before he could push it to the magic goal.

The grinding pace of all those seasons played on a dead run would take its toll. He would hang on until the 1970s, returning to New York to finish his career with the Mets. But he, too, would finally be beaten by age and time.

Only "Bad Henry" would survive.

By the summer of 1973, with Ruth's record clearly in sight, Henry Aaron was the most famous athlete in America.

There was no longer a way to ignore him. He had arrived at the gates of baseball immortality. He would break the unbreakable record.

As far back as 1968, he had firmly established himself as one of the best home run hitters in baseball. On July 14 of that year, batting in Atlanta against Mike McCormick of the San Francisco Giants, he rapped a drive off the scoreboard for the 500th home run of his career.

He had entered a special group. He was numbered among the greats. But more importantly, at the age of 34, with the possibility of several seasons still ahead, he was seen as a real threat to Ruth's record.

He played it down when people asked about it. He told reporters that it wasn't on his mind. He said he was just going out to hit the ball, and if a home run came, then a home run came.

He said he didn't want anyone to forget Babe Ruth; he only wanted them to remember Henry Aaron.

There was nothing more, not publicly, only his intent to play the game as best he could.

But on the field, his performance spoke of a mission.

Over the next three years, he set a torrid pace. He hit 44 home runs in 1969, added another 39 in 1970, then produced an all-time personal high of 47 in 1971.

He hit Number 600 in April. He hit it off Gaylord Perry of the San Francisco Giants.

But in 1972, he had an off year. There were problems with the front office and problems on the field. His throwing arm was fading fast, so he switched to first base. He felt awkward and uncomfortable in the new position. His defensive play was poor.

He hit only .265, batting in 77 runs. Yet he still managed to hit 34 homers.

He was criticized by some. There were those who said he was more interested in breaking the record than he was in helping the Braves to win.

But Aaron said little in response. He was defended by his friend and manager, Eddie Mathews, and as the 1973 season grew near, the criticism faded. The baseball world watched and waited.

The record was within his reach, but did he have the strength to take it?

He was 39 years old and his arm was gone. He was coming off a bad season, terrible by his standards. Would age and time take him the same way they took Mays?

He responded with an amazing season. As the country marked his progress day by day, with the commotion mounting and the pressure building to a peak, he blasted 40 home runs and batted .301.

By the end of the season, he had hit 713 career home runs. It was only a matter of time. The record would fall.

And on the night it did, on the night that he hit the 715th home run of his major league career, Henry Aaron became the king of home run hitters. But he became something more as well.

He became a legend.

Someday in the future, when Americans look back on the era, they may remember a man who came at a time when spirits were low. The American people were confused and frightened. They were sick of war. They did not trust their government, and they did not trust their neighbors. There was fear and poverty, and crime in the streets.

It was a time when Americans were in search of something they had lost, a purpose and a direction built on the ideals of freedom and equality. They had no inspiration. There was no real sign that the country was good and fair and strong, that it was the country they believed in.

They were in need of a hero.

He came to them that night in Atlanta, on national television, when with one sure stroke of his bat, he scaled the highest mountain. In a white man's game, with white men's rules, he played for the biggest prize in American sport. He played it for himself, and he won.

And for this, he was cheered. He was admired and honored, decorated and rewarded. He was taken at his value as a man of deeds.

Yes, there were those who begrudged him. There were those who mailed him messages of hate, who called him names from their seats in the stands. But he withstood them silently, with courage and pride, with a firm belief in himself.

And in the end, he was accepted.

He did not heal a nation's wounds. He did not bring a divided people together, joining them in the spirit of brotherhood. He did not signal a time when racial injustice was no more.

But he contributed.

Quietly, in his own way, he brought them a gift. At a time in their history when heroes were few, he brought them an image.

In its reflection, life looked just a little brighter.

He showed them a man of dignity and honor, of courage and dedication. He showed them a man of pride.

46

He is the sum total of the best part of 200 years of American history.

He is the true American hero.

Design   **Interface Design Group Inc.**